Sand
and
Water
Play

A space to learn

Anne Pratt

corner to Learn

“To my grandchildren Matthew, James, Ben and Ruby for all the fun we have together and for a great excuse to keep on playing.”

Sand and Water Play

Published by
Corner to Learn Limited
Willow Cottage, 26 Purton Stoke
Swindon, Wiltshire SN5 4JF, UK

www.cornertolearn.co.uk

ISBN 978-1-905434-19-0

Text © Anne Pratt 2007

First edition

British Library Cataloguing-in-Publication Data. A catalogue record for this book is available from the British Library.

Series Editor
Neil Griffiths

Editor
Francesca Pinagli

Design
David Rose

Printed by
Tien Wah Press Pte. Ltd., Singapore

Contents

"What picture is conjured up for you when the word 'sand tray' is mentioned? Endless sieving? Continuous digging and pointless filling? For some teachers, the very idea of sand brings on a headache and a fearful dread of the cleaner's reaction at the end of the day! Typical adult responses include: 'It's too messy.' 'It takes up so much room.' 'We don't have enough time.' 'I can never think of enough activities.' Its very inclusion in a classroom can lead to fears that it will become an opportunity for children to become noisy and disruptive. However, most early years practitioners would feel guilty at removing the sand trays and they can often be found lurking somewhere in a classroom, even if infrequently used, filled with an inch of sand and in a dark corner.

This book aims to shed fresh light on the value of sand play and inspire practitioners to recognise its unique role in developing the whole child and the contribution it can make to their early years."

Neil Griffiths
Series editor

Introduction

Few young children can resist playing with water, sand, mud or other similar materials. Take a walk after a rainstorm and most young children will seek out puddles to splash in. Try to do the washing-up and, suddenly, there are eager little helpers at your elbow. Go to do some gardening and someone is just behind you doing their own bit of digging. Play with these materials is very absorbing, great fun and is full of opportunity for addressing every area of the Foundation curriculum.

Play with sand and water helps children's **physical** development. Through lifting, pouring, sieving, sifting, filling, emptying and handling these materials, children learn to control movement, particularly those movements requiring careful hand and eye coordination. Filling one container from another can be quite tricky and requires a lot of practice.

Play with sand and water is pleasurable. It is calming and relaxing to explore the feel, smell,

and movement of these materials, and through doing this, children make discoveries. They learn how the materials behave in different situations and begin to understand that, for example, sand behaves differently when it is wet from when it is dry. Wet sand can be moulded and shaped, while dry sand behaves a bit like water and can flow and be moved easily. They discover that some things float on water, while others sink. They find out that materials sometimes change in certain conditions; water can become ice, for example; too much water in the sand and you won't be able to mould it; put lots of stones in your bucket of water and it will overflow. These are all important steps towards later **scientific** understanding.

With help from adults, children learn a wide range of new vocabulary. Some of the language will be essential to their understanding in **Maths**. Words such as *full, empty, half full, half empty, more, less, fewer, big, little*, etc. will naturally come into conversation. There are lots of opportunities for counting in this play, for example, *How many spoonfuls of sand fill the cup? How many sand castles have you made? Can you put three flags on your castle?*

Two or three children playing together around a sand or water tray will learn a lot about getting on with others. They will have to share, exchange ideas, take turns and **communicate** with one another.

This book aims to help Early Years practitioners take sand and water play out of the dark corner of the room where it sometimes resides as a *time filler* with little clear purpose and rarely visited by adults. However, with a little careful planning and some time and thought given to the organisation, the resources and the involvement of adults, sand and water play can provide all the following opportunities for young children to:

- explore and investigate materials and their properties
- have different sensory experiences
- develop creativity and imagination
- encourage scientific exploration
- increase vocabulary and stimulate discussion
- develop mathematical language and concepts
- reinforce learning in other areas of the curriculum
- follow a theme or topic
- develop hand-eye coordination
- experience therapeutic and soothing materials
- learn to work and play with others, sharing resources and ideas
- get messy
- have fun!

1 Getting organised

Containers

- No matter how small or difficult your space, there is always a way to provide some satisfying play with natural materials. There are many smart sand and water trays on the market – what you buy will be governed by your budget, the space available and the age of the children. If you only have a small budget and little space, sand and water play in baby baths, plastic boxes, seed trays, paint roller trays and plant trays can be just as satisfying as play in the latest smart container from an educational catalogue.

- When buying a tray from a catalogue, carefully consider the following questions:

  - What shape fits best in the space available?
  - Will it be easy to empty and keep clean?
  - Is the height right for the age of the children in the group? (You may need a tray with two levels within in it so that everyone can reach the sand / water.)
  - Do I need a tray with some storage space underneath for resources?

Where to put the play

- If possible, keep sand and water play on an easily-cleaned, non-slip surface. If you have no such area, try using non-slip shower mats around the trays.

- Try not to site water and sand trays too near to one another. The urge to mix these two materials is very strong in young children and all you will end up with is two very wet, sandy puddles in both trays!

- Put the water tray as near to a source of water as you can. A small length of hose that can be easily attached to a tap is helpful for filling a water tray.

- If you intend putting the sand play outside in fine weather, put the tray as near to a door as possible and make sure that if it is left outside, it is covered.

- Try not to hide it away in a dark corner where it will be easily overlooked and have no status in your setting.

Getting started with resources
Basic needs

- Some basic resources will be appropriate for play in both sand and water. Funnels, sieves, buckets, jugs, cups, spoons, etc. are suitable for both. Many cheap or redundant household bits and pieces make ideal resources for sand and water play.

- Make sure you have enough resources so that the children do not squabble or become frustrated. Make sure there is sufficient sand to make the play worthwhile. Make sure the water is sparkling clean.

- These basic resources will initially provide absorbing play. Basic materials such as spades, buckets, sieves, jugs, spoons, etc. can be hung conveniently near the play area and lend themselves well to shadow labelling, which provides a great way for children to learn to put things away and also develops matching skills.

- Use blue boxes for water resources and yellow boxes for sand resources. Sometimes it is possible to find clear plastic boxes (these are better for seeing into) with blue or yellow lids. This colour coding makes for easier identification for both staff and children.

What resources will I need?

- plastic containers of all sizes
- plastic plant pots
- colanders
- plastic pipes (e.g. pieces of guttering or similar), plastic tubing
- straws
- well-cleaned washing-up liquid bottles and spray containers (e.g. window cleaner spray)
- rubber gloves
- bubble pipes
- corks
- liquid soap pumps

Building up resource collections

- Initially, children will enjoy and learn from playing freely with the conventional range of resources. They will enjoy sieving, pouring, moulding, etc. and will be learning from these experiences, but practioners will need to observe the play carefully and be aware when children need new challenges and fresh resources and ideas to explore. Challenge can come from both adult intervention and questioning and from new things to explore.

- Put together collections which focus on one particular idea or skill.

Collections might be made to encourage the following themes:

Sand themes

For making patterns and pictures in sand, several boxes could be put together, each containing a different selection of resources. More specific pattern-making could be developed by putting together resources that encourage:

- holes and tunnels in sand
- pouring and filling with sand
- looking at sand, feeling sand
- moulding and modelling with sand
- moving sand
- sand play outdoors

Water themes

- holes and water
- siphons and pumps
- sprays and jets
- making bubbles
- repelling water
- fish and fishing
- toys that move in water
- pouring and filling
- moving water
- floating and sinking
- absorbing water
- bath toys
- water play outdoors

Holes and tunnels:

- Children will enjoy exploring unusual, unfamiliar objects. Many things can be found around the home, but make sure they are perfectly clean and free from sharp edges.

- Many of the things that you will put into the boxes are easily and inexpensively collected. For example holes and tunnels in sand might include:
  - A variety of tubes and pipes of different shapes and sizes (bits often found in builder's merchants and DIY stores)
  - Funnels
  - Sieves
  - Flowerpots
  - Kitchen equipment such as colanders, slotted spoons, strainers, garlic crushers, etc.

Moving water:

- Moving water might include:
  - Pumps (Some well cleaned household pumps from soap, washing-up liquid etc. make useful resources.)
  - Sprays (again sometimes found in the home)
  - Pipes, gutters, hoses, straws
  - Water wheels
  - A range of containers such as buckets, bowls, scoops, spoons, bottles, cups, a teapot, jugs

Further collections:

- Other collections which provide interesting opportunities for investigation in the water are:
  - natural collections
  - a collection of plastic bottles in a variety of shapes and sizes
  - a collection of bottles with holes in the side
  - a collection of cleaning brushes, e.g. nail brushes, bottle brushes, scrubbing brushes, washing-up brushes, toothbrushes, etc. (it's great fun to scrub and clean plastic toys and plastic construction sets and the like.)
  - a collection of paint brushes of different thicknesses and lengths (These are great for water play outside.)
  - a collection of different-shaped and sized sponges and cloths

- Having your resources well sorted and clearly labelled will make it easier to present different challenges and ideas to the children.
- Remember, further interest, variety and learning can be introduced by changing the texture of the sand - sometimes it can be damp, sometimes wet and sometimes it can be left dry; water can be changed by adding colour, ice, bubbles, making it warm or leaving it cold. Adding plastic bags of coloured water that can be punctured, will allow the children to observe the dilution of the colours and the patterns that are made. **However, do not use washing-up liquid to make bubbles in the water as it can cause adverse skin reactions in children. Use a safe and gentle baby bath liquid such as *Infacare*. Also, always take care when using plastic bags.**

Collections for imaginative play in sand and water

Imaginative play in sand and water can also be encouraged through collections. Decide on a few basic sets around themes and stories and store the sets in plastic boxes or baskets, labelled with text and pictures so that they are easily recognised and accessed.

Suggestions for collections

- Dinosaurs
- Building and construction
- The jungle
- The seaside
- Pirates
- Creepie crawlies
- Woodland and woodland creatures
- The farm
- The park
- The garden
- Castles
- The airport
- The town / city

Excellent resources for these sets can be brought inexpensively from stores such as *Woolworth, Asda* and the *Early Learning Centre.*

Rules for sand and water play

Both children and Early Years practitioners need to abide by some rules for sand and water play.

Rules for adults

- Make the area as exciting and as attractive as possible.
- Keep the sand and water scrupulously clean.
- Change the water every day and make sure the sand has no undesirable bits and pieces in it!
- Check tools and resources regularly as cracked, split, damaged plastic can hurt small hands.
- Make sure there is sufficient sand to make the play worthwhile and that there are enough tools for everyone to be able to take part.
- Make sure there is planned time for adults to be in this area, observing the play and working with the children.

- Ensure that it is the children who clear up after each session and not the adults. (So ensure that equipment such as dust pans and brushes are stored close by.)
- Store equipment and resources attractively and make them easy to access.
- Make sure aprons are available in the area.

The photo on the right is an example of aprons simply and easily stored:
- Velcro strip on the wall.
- Aprons with small velcro strip.
- Easy to attach the two together, simple to collect, put away and keep tidy.

Rules for children

- Talk with the children about rules for sand and water play. Ask them to think of things that will help make the play safe and enjoyable. Write the rules on a poster and display these in the sand and water area. Pictures will help children to remember what these are. They should include:

Please do not throw sand.

Remember to put an apron on.

Keep sand away from your face

Be careful! Always remember to walk, not run, in the sand and water area.

Please help to tidy up and put things away in the right place.

2 Planning sand and water play

Play is most successful when children are provided with a real purpose for their play, a stimulating starting point and attractive interesting resources.

Points to consider when planning

- possible starting points and links to other areas of the Foundation curriculum
- the selection and quality of the resources
- the needs, development and interests of the children
- the time available for the play
- the opportunities for adult intervention and interaction
- the opportunities for assessment and those who will be responsible for doing this

- Some Early Years practioners may wish to record their plans for sand and water play on separate sheets which can be displayed in the play area. This helps to inform parents and other adults of the value of the play, gives helpers a clear idea of what is going on and what the aims and objectives are. See pages 14 and 15 for examples of planning sheets.

- From time to time, adults will need to spend some time in the sand and water area, observing progress and behaviour and recording milestones in development. Many Early Years settings now plan much of their work around children's schema. Schema are children's learning behaviour patterns and many Early Years settings identify these patterns through careful observation of the children, then plan work which nourishes, enriches and develops their schema. The study of children's schema is fascinating.

There are several excellent publications relating to children's schema. Among these are:

Extending thought in young children, C. Athey (Paul Chapman)

Threads of thinking, Cathy Nutbrown (Paul Chapman)

Child Development and Learning 2-5 Years - Georgina's Story, C. Arnold (Hodder and Stoughton)

Early Childhood Education, Tina Bruce (Hodder and Stoughton)

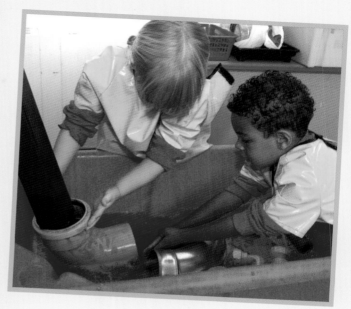

- Sand and water play has many opportunities for children to follow their schema. For example, in sand and water play, some of the more common schema can be planned for by providing the following resources and activities:

Connection schema

- funnels and bottles
- tunnels
- pipes
- tubes
- hoses
- bridges

Enveloping and enclosure schema

- burying things - feet, treasure and other objects
- making tunnels
- filling things with sand and water - bags, pots, pipes, funnels
- blowing bubbles
- making boats

Trajectory schema

- digging, using things with holes such as sieves, colanders, etc.
- making straight line patterns and pictures in sand
- pipes and guttering
- in the water - bubbles, pipes, pumps, sprays, squeezy bottles
- in large outdoor sand areas, walking through sand, making large trails, lifting sand with pulleys

Transporting schema

- sand in pipes, gutters, vehicles
- making trails in the sand
- pouring sand and transporting it from one area to another
- transporting sand to water, and vice versa
- in the water, hose pipes, guttering, pouring water
- moving water from one container to another

Rotation schema

- sand wheels and sprinklers
- making circular patterns and pictures in the sand
- pushing wheeled vehicles through sand
- water wheels, whisks, stirring and sprinkling

- For those groups who plan work through this approach, part of their observations and assessment procedures will be noting and recording individual children's schema.

- On the following pages are two examples of planning sheets which you may be able to adapt to your needs.

Sand and Water Sample Planning Sheet

Planning: Exploring moving sand. A progression for several play sessions.

Teaching and learning: Language, Manipulation skills, Ability to share, Solving problems

Focus	Teaching and learning	Play opportunity	Resources	Adult interaction	Assessment, Examples
Exploring how sand moves through holes	Developing knowledge and understanding of: • The way dry sand behaves, making comparisons, observing how sand flows through holes, speed, action, and pattern	Free exploration of resources: • Making patterns with sieved sand • Exploring speed of emptying and sieving	Dry sand: • A collection of sieves, colanders, funnels, mill wheels, etc. • Small spades and scoops	• Allow child-led time to explore. • Encourage children to observe how dry sand moves through holes in sieves / when full / empty / speed / patterns. • Questions: Which sieve empties the quickest? etc.	How involved are they in activities? Do they need further challenges? Can they use language correctly? Do they need more experience with language?
Moving sand by pouring, filling and emptying	Develop mathematical understanding of: • *Full, empty, nearly full, half full / empty* and shape	Free exploration of resources: • Pouring and filling • Picnic scenario – filling cups, etc.	Dry sand: • A collection of plastic containers, different sizes and shapes • Picnic set	• Allow child-led time to explore. • Work with containers. • Fill and empty completely. • Use language: *empty, full, half full, big, small*, etc. • Suggest filling with funnel and tube.	Do they understand the language and concepts introduced? Do they need more time in the different contexts? Can sizes be differentiated? Can they fill containers? Do they need more time to explore?
Exploring ways that dry sand can be made to flow	Developing knowledge and understanding of: • Dry sand will flow downhill, can be speeded up / slowed down by changing angle of slope. • Dry sand flows like water	Free play with resources: • Moving sand from one level to another • Exploring sand flow, speed, etc.	Dry sand in two containers: • A collection of plastic piping, guttering of varying sizes, narrow and wide bore tubes • Funnels and other pouring containers	• Allow child-led time to explore. • Add varying sizes of guttering. • Explore ways to make dry sand flow faster or slower.	Can they find what will move sand quickest / slowest? Can they describe slope? Can they say what is happening? Can they tell what makes sand start to move? Do they need more experience?
Comparing how dry and wet sand differ in the way they move	Developing knowledge and understanding of: • Difference between moving wet and dry sand • Making comparisons • Using appropriate words to describe, explain and predict	Encourage free play with resources with both wet and dry sand: • Fill containers with dry sand • Play with dry sand on guttering • Fill containers with wet sand • Compare	• Two trays, one with wet sand the other with dry sand • Other resources as above	• Allow child-led time to explore. • Encourage prediction, e.g. What might happen to wet sand / dry sand in the sieve and in the guttering? • Explore these ideas and any others raised by the activity.	Can they say why wet / dry sand behave differently? Can they talk about their observations?
Imaginative play around theme of the building site (See Sandscapes Set 2 for ideas and extending this activity.)	Developing: • Imagination • Story telling • Co-operation	• Creating an imaginative Building Site • Making up stories about play • Investigating different toy vehicles and their properties	• Trays of damp sand • Collection of toy vehicles found on building sites, e.g. lorries, diggers, rollers, tractors, trailers • Small figures • Small sand tools	• Talk about / visit building sites, use a story / pictures • Allow child-led time then discuss functions of vehicles and the effect in moving sand. • Make up stories.	Can they play in the sand imaginatively? Do they co-operate with one another? Can they tell a story?

Sand and Water Planning Sheet

Planning:
Teaching and learning:

Focus	Teaching and learning	Play opportunity	Resources	Adult interaction	Assessment, Examples

The involvement of adults

Plan for adults to spend some time with the children in the sand and water play area. This will vastly improve the quality of the play and give opportunities for:

- modelling the play - playing alongside the children and sometimes initiating play
- extending vocabulary
- asking questions to extend ideas and challenge the children
- giving praise and encouragement
- intervening
- ensuring rules are kept
- assessing when new ideas and resources need to be introduced
- observing individual children and making assessments of their:
    - use of vocabulary and language skills
    - ability to follow instructions
    - levels of concentration
    - ability to make decisions
    - manipulative skills
    - ability to ask questions
    - degree of independence
    - social skills
    - understanding of mathematical and scientific concepts

> " The involvement of an adult in play is crucial if the children are to feel their efforts are appreciated. "

- Play with sand and water will give children many opportunities to learn new words and their meanings. Here are just a few that might be introduced during this play. It is useful to display these words in areas where adults are working so that they can refer to and use the words as prompts in their interaction with the children.

Words relating to feeling sand

coarse	rough
gritty	smooth
wet	dry
damp	cold
grainy	granular
slushy	fine

Words relating to things that happen with water

drip	drop
splash	trickle
swirl	whirl
squirt	spray
pump	siphon
swish	float
sink	absorb
repel	dissolve
gush	gurgle
freeze	melt
bubbles	plop
ripple	dribble
pour	filter

Scientific and mathematical words

empty	full
half empty	half full
level	waterproof
more	less

Words relating to actions with sand

push	sieve
pat	sift
press	trickle
mould	dig
shape	excavate
squeeze	flow
shake	pile
sprinkle	rake
comb	pour
drizzle	scoop
tunnel	print

Words relating to the feel of water

cold	hot
freezing	warm
icy	soapy
foamy	smooth
squelchy	slushy

Mathematical words

full	empty
half full	half empty
more	less
bigger	smaller
higher	taller
few	many
flat	round
fast	slow
heavy	light

3 Ourselves

 Starting point

Hands and the sense of touch

- A topic frequently developed with young children in the pre-school, nursery or reception class.

What resources will I need?

- Initially, take all the tools out of the sand and water and let the children explore these materials by just using their hands. The sand can be changed so that sometimes it is dry, sometimes wet, sometimes damp. Water can be cold or warm.

Main activity

- Fill a large sand tray or several small trays with damp sand. Encourage the children to mould and shape the damp sand with their hands and make patterns with their hands and fingers. Encourage the children to talk about what they are doing and how the sand feels. Introduce new vocabulary such as *mould*, *smooth* and *shape*.

- In the water tray, let the children trickle water through their hands and fingers, splash and move water with their hands. Talk to the children about how this feels and introduce vocabulary such as *trickle*, *scoop*, *splash*, *make waves*.

Extending the activity

- When the children have thoroughly explored this activity, introduce sieves, funnels and sand wheels so that when the sand is dry, they can feel the sand as it passes through these things. Put water wheels, jugs, sponges and funnels in the water so that they can do the same.
- Let small groups of children make a *feely trail in* the sand by burying small, differently textured objects in the sand (fir cones, bubble wrap, beads, Lego pieces, stickle bricks, etc.) and invite their friends to feel for the treasures and identify them.
- Put stones, sponges, loofahs and shells into the water so that the children can see and feel the difference between them when they are dry and wet.

Further extension

- Put other natural materials in individual seed trays so that the children can experience the feel of these. You can use sawdust, wood shavings, shredded paper, gravel, stones, shells, porridge oats, etc. Play a guessing game once they are familiar with the feel and texture of these. Include damp, dry and wet sand in the range of materials. Blindfold the children and ask them to guess what they are feeling. Note that some children are afraid of blindfolds, so be aware of this when asking children to take part.
- Put some ice into water in small bowls so that the children can feel the different stages of melting.
- **Always be aware of the allergies that your children may suffer from.**

Poems, stories and rhymes

- Teach the children a variety of finger rhymes.

  This Little Puffin, Elizabeth Matterson (Puffin Books) is a good source for these.
  My Hands, Aliki, (Harper Collins) - part of the *Lets read and Find Out* Science series
  What do I touch?, Harrriet Ziefert (Collins)

When we were babies
Bathing the baby

- This is often part of a topic relating to Ourselves, but could equally be included as part of Hospital play, Domestic corner play or play relating to the Baby clinic. If possible, invite a parent with a new baby to come and talk about bath time and to show the children how the baby is bathed.

What resources will I need?

- baby bath or a small water tray
- warm water
- bath thermometer
- dolls which will stand up to frequent bathing
- towels
- aprons
- table with a baby changing mat
- baby bath bubbles
- sponge
- face cloth
- baby wipes
- baby bath toys
- basket containing cotton wool, cotton buds, hair brush, baby shampoo (Put only the tiniest bit for each group in a bottle!)
- empty pot of cream
- doll's clothes
- nappy

Main activity

Discuss bath time with the children and their experience of babies being bathed. Talk about safety issues such as water temperature, avoiding soap in the eyes, the need to be gentle and careful with babies. Demonstrate baby bathing techniques with a doll if you have been unable to get a parent to bring a real baby in. Introduce new vocabulary such as *temperature*, *thermometer* and *delicate*. Name the equipment to be used. Talk about its purpose.

Key learning opportunities

Communication, language and literacy

- Extend vocabulary.
- Use language to recreate roles and experiences.
- Use talk to clarify and express ideas and feelings.
- Interact with others.

Personal, social and emotional development

- Work as part of a group.
- Be confident to try new activities.
- Be interested and excited and motivated to learn.

Knowledge and understanding

- Explore new materials using the senses.
- Find out about the world we live in.

Physical development

- Handle tools and objects with increasing control.

Creative development

- Play imaginatively.

Extending the activity

- Provide a collection of different sized feeding bottles and measuring jugs, spoons and scoops. Let the children pretend they are mixing feeds for the baby. This involves lots of pouring and filling and a high degree of hand-eye coordination. It is an excellent opportunity for practising counting skills and introducing vocabulary such as *full, empty, half full, half empty, more, less*.

Poems, stories and rhymes

- To the tune of *Here we go round the mulberry bush*, sing:

  This is the way we bath the baby,
  bath the baby, bath the baby.
  This the way we bath the baby
  on a cold and frosty morning.
  This is the way we wash her hair,
  wash her hair, wash her hair, etc.

- Play and teach nursery rhymes such as *This Little Piggy went to Market*.

  Read stories about babies. There are many available. Here is a small selection:
  The world is full of babies, Mick Manning and Britta Granstrom (Franklin Watts Books)
  New Born, Kathy Henderson (Frances Lincoln)
  Bye Bye Baby, Janet and Alan Alhberg (Puffin Books)
  Nothing, Mick Inkpen (Hodder Children's Books)

Washing clothes

- Stories can be included as part of play relating to the Home corner.

  Mrs Mopple's Washing Line, Anita Hewitt and Robert Broomfield (Red Fox)

  Doing the Washing, Sarah Garland (Bodley Head Children's Books)

  There was an old woman who lived in a shoe (nursery rhyme)

What resources will I need?

- water tray
- bowls or a baby bath filled with warm water
- aprons
- a very gentle soapy mixture (Do not use washing powders as some children are allergic to these and they may cause skin rashes.)
- washing basket
- pegs
- line or clothes horse for the clothes
- nail brush
- selection of clothes to wash (Possibly dolls' clothes or a selection of no longer used children's and adults' clothes. Try to provide an interesting collection which lends itself to sorting and some discussion relating to size, colour, shape and pattern.)

Main activity

- Start with a story such as Sarah Garland's *Doing the Washing*. Look at a basket of washing with the children. What do they already know about washing clothes? Do they ever help at home? Talk about the importance of sorting colours and whites. Talk about the fabrics, colours, patterns and sizes of the clothes. This is a brilliant activity for developing mathematical language and assessing children's understanding of mathematical ideas relating to size, shape and pattern.

- If the weather is warm and you have the space, put this activity outside. Put up a washing line that the children can easily reach. They will get very wet, so make sure they have aprons. If they are outside, wellington boots help to keep feet dry.

Key learning opportunities

Communication, language and literacy

- Use language to imagine and recreate roles and experiences.
- Use talk to sequence, organise and clarify thinking, ideas, feelings and events.
- Ask and answer questions.
- Extend vocabulary, learning meanings and sounds of new words.

Personal, social and emotional development

- Be confident to try new activities.
- Work as part of a group, taking turns and sharing.
- Select and use resources independently.

Mathematical development

- Say and use number names in order.
- Count to ten.
- In practical activities, use language such as *more than*.

- Begin to use and understand comparisons such as *longer than*, *bigger than*, *smaller*.

Knowledge and understanding

- Investigate objects and materials using all senses.
- Look closely at similarities and differences, patterns and change.
- Talk about how things work.
- Find out about everyday technology (washing machines).

Physical development

- Handle tools and objects with increasing control. (Pegging out washing requires a high degree of manipulative dexterity.)

Creative development

- Play imaginatively.
- Explore shape, colour and pattern.

Extending the activity

- Talk about washing long ago. Show the children pictures of old-fashioned irons, dolly tubs and other equipment. You may be lucky enough to have access to a resource centre or a parent who can provide you with a collection of old washing equipment. The children may be able to use these to do some washing.

- Set up the role play area as a launderette (*A Corner to Learn*, Neil Griffiths (Nelson Thornes) for ideas on how to do this). Extend the home corner play by introducing washing equipment. Conduct some experiments based around drying time. Ask the children to sort the washing into those things which will dry first and those which will take a long time.

- Extend sorting activities. Put a collection of socks into pairs. Introduce sets of clothing, e.g. nightwear, swimwear, underwear. Ask the children to hang the washing out in sets or, as in the case of socks, in pairs. *Stepping Stones 'Ourselves' Teacher's Book*, (Nelson Thornes) page 37 and 38 has good suggestions for activities around doing the washing.

Poems, stories and rhymes

- To the tune of *Here we go round the mulberry bush*, sing *This is the way we wash our clothes*. This is an excellent way of getting children to put procedures connected with washing into a correct sequence.

  Rub a dub dub.
  I'm forever blowing bubbles.
  Sorting socks (You will find this sorting rhyme in *The Stepping Stones Big Book 'Ourselves'* (Nelson Thornes)

Bathing and bath toys

Starting point

- Exploring bath toys could be an extension of the activities related to Bathing the baby or as a part of a topic around Toys. It is an excellent way of encouraging children to explore the idea of floating and sinking, pumps and sprays, simple mechanisms such as clockwork and water wheels, making things move in water and the delights of making and blowing bubbles.

What resources will I need?

- collection of boats of different types – some big, some small
- collection of ducks – some big, some small
- collection of wind-up bath toys – boats, frogs, sea creatures, etc.
- water wheel
- bath toys which work on the water wheel principle
- toys which can be made to spray and squirt water – toy whale, fire boats, etc.
- toys which work using a pumping mechanism
- waterproof bath books
- collection of plastic sea creatures
- collection of plastic people
- bubble blowers and gentle bubble solution
- water tray or baby bath
- warm water
- aprons

A selection of different bath toys can be found in most toy shops, but why not ask the children to bring in their favourites? These would make an interesting display and a great talking point.

Main activity

- Give the children a small selection of the toys or just one particular set such as the clockwork toys or the boats. Let the children experiment with these, finding out what they will do. When the children have had a good opportunity to play freely with the toys, allocate an adult to the area to ask questions and extend learning. How do the children think a particular toy works? Can they describe how it moves? Can they make it sink? Can they think of other things that work in this way? Can they make the non-mechanised toys move in the water? Encourage the children to put the toys into sets based on how they work and move, for example, toys which move mechanically; toys which float.

Key learning opportunities

Communication, language and literacy

- Extend vocabulary, explore the meaning and sound of new words.
- Interact with others and take turns in conversation.
- Use talk to clarify ideas and express feelings.
- Ask and answer questions.

Personal, social and emotional development

- Work together as a group.
- Listen to the ideas of others.

Mathematical development

- Learn and use mathematical vocabulary such as *bigger, smaller, more than, less than*.
- Sort and classify objects.

- Count to ten.
- Begin to use and understand comparisons such as *longer than, bigger than, smaller*.

Knowledge and understanding

- Explore some aspects of technology – wheels, propellers, clockwork.
- Find out how things work and ask questions about why things happen.
- Explore, through practical activities, scientific concepts such as floating and sinking and water as a force.

Physical development

- Learn to control small movement such as winding up clockwork toys.

- Introduce vocabulary such as *clockwork, mechanical, floating, sinking, squirting, pumping*, and so on. Talk about scientific ideas such as floating and sinking and the force of water turning mechanisms such as wheels and propellers.

- Introduce mathematical vocabulary such as *bigger, smaller, more than, less than* and use every opportunity for counting and sorting. For example, how many ducks are in the water, how many are small, how many are large? Are there more small ducks or more large ducks?

Extending the activity

- Introduce different sets of bath toys. Ask the children if they can guess how they work by just looking at them. Set challenges such as *Can you guess how long the clockwork frog will swim in the water before he stops?* Use egg timers for this and get the children to make estimates such as: *before the egg timer runs out, once, two goes of the egg timer*, and so on.

Poems, stories and rhymes

Five little ducks went swimming one day; *Row, row, row your boat* and other similar rhymes can be found in **This Little Puffin**, Elizabeth Matterson (Penguin Books)
Mr Gumpy's Outing, John Burningham (Red Fox) (A good story to use with the idea of floating and sinking and to play out with boats and animals.)
The Journey, Neil Griffiths (Red Robin Books) (The story of the journey of a little boy's boat from the river to the sea.)

Birthdays

Making birthday cakes in the sand

- Birthdays are often part of a topic relating to Ourselves, but could equally be included as part of a topic relating to Food, Celebrations or a story such as **Spot goes to a party**, Eric Hill (Frederick Warne) or **Coming to Tea**, Sarah Garland (Puffin Books).

What resources will I need?

- sand tray
- plenty of damp sand
- different sized and shaped cake tins and bun tins. (Metal tins must not be left in damp sand as they quickly corrode. Different sized and shaped plastic cake storage boxes would be a better option.)
- plastic / wooden spoons of different sizes
- plastic bowls
- plastic straws cut into candle-sized lengths
- cake decorations suitable for putting into the sand (i.e. preferably plastic, but glass marbles, shells and other natural materials make good decoration for sand cakes.)

Main activity

- After talking about birthday parties and birthday cakes, show the children the resources that you have collected for them to use in the sand. Suggest they make several cakes and decorate them. Talk about the candles and ask the children to decide what age their cake / cakes are to be for. Talk about the consistency of the sand and ask them to suggest what it should be like to make successful moulds. Ask questions relating to the size and shape of their cakes. Ask them to count the candles and write the number in the sand. Suggest that they show their sand cakes to other groups of children before they are demolished.

Key learning opportunities

Communication, language and literacy

- Extend vocabulary.
- Use language to recreate roles and experiences
- Use talk to clarify and express ideas and feelings.
- Interact with others.

Personal, social and emotional development

- Work as part of a group.
- Be confident to try new activities.
- Be interested and excited and motivated to learn.
- Understand about important events in our lives and the lives of others.

Mathematical development

- Count reliably to ten.
- Talk about and recognise different shapes and patterns.
- Learn vocabulary such as *bigger than, more than, as big as*, and so on.

Knowledge and understanding

- Explore new materials using senses.
- Find out about the world we live in.

Physical development

- Handle tools and objects with increasing control.

Creative development

- Play imaginatively.

Extending the activity

- Put jelly moulds of different shapes and sizes in the sand. Let the children make moulds with these.
- Concentrate the water play around the theme of party drinks. Provide jugs of different sizes, small bowls, plastic beakers, food colouring and a selection of plastic fruits. Colour the water and let the children mix drinks, pour and fill. Stress that they must not try to drink their concoctions.
- Look at **Stepping Stones Teacher's Book 'Ourselves'**, (Nelson Thornes) for lots of good ideas relating to play around the theme of Birthdays.

Poems, stories and rhymes

Sing birthday party rhymes such as *Oranges and Lemons, Here we go round the mulberry bush* and *Farmer's in his Den*.

- Read stories such as:

  Spot's Birthday Party and
  Spot goes to a Party, Eric Hill
  (Frederick Warne)
  It's my Birthday, Helen Oxenbury
  (Walker Books)
  Happy Birthday, Sam, Pat Hutchins
  (Red Fox)

4 Gardens

Starting point

Creating a Garden

- This is another popular theme explored with young children. It offers many opportunities for sand and water play. It is often explored as part of a theme relating to Growth, Changes, the Seasons, Minibeasts or after a visit to a garden or a garden centre. There are a number of stories or rhymes which also make excellent starting points.

What resources will I need?

- large sand tray or small individual trays (Seed trays or paint roller trays are big enough for one child to create their own special garden.)
- small tools for digging, moulding and creating patterns (Small garden tools would be ideal – trowels, forks, rakes, sieves, etc. – all available in child sizes.)
- collection of materials for creating flowers, shrubs, hedges, bushes, trees and vegetables: small artificial flowers, model trees, green wool, pan scourers, artificial grass, green plastic, coloured paper and a selection of natural greenery and plants
- small stones and pebbles for creating paths, walls and for edging beds
- small pots for creating tubs
- sticks and pieces of wood to use as supports for making plants
- plastic containers for creating a pond or, if you are concerned about too much water in the sand, shiny paper such as tinfoil to create an illusion of water

Key learning opportunities

Communication, language and literacy

- Use language to imagine and recreate roles and experiences.
- Use talk to sequence, organise and clarify thinking, ideas, feelings and events.
- Ask and answer questions.
- Extend vocabulary, learning meanings and sounds of new words.

Personal, social and emotional development

- Be confident to try new activities.
- Work as part of a group, taking turns and sharing.
- Select and use resources independently.

Knowledge and understanding

- Investigate objects and materials using all senses.
- Look closely at similarities and differences, patterns and change.

Physical development

- Handle tools and objects with increasing control.

Creative development

- Play imaginatively.
- Explore shape, colour and pattern.

Main activity

- Talk about gardens and the children's own experience of them. Look at some garden magazines and other pictures of gardens. (**Gardens Illustrated** always has beautiful photographs of different gardens in different settings.)
- Record children's ideas about what can be in a garden on a flip chart. Look at the resources and discuss ways that they can be used. Display pictures, magazines and books about gardens so that the children can access these for inspiration and information.

Extending the activity

- Talk about, visit and look at pictures of other types of gardens: Japanese gardens, parks, gardens at home, allotments.
- Look at ideas for the whole theme of gardens in **Stepping Stones**, (Nelson Thornes). There is a wealth of ideas in the teachers book and posters and a big book to support work in this area.
- Look at the ideas in the **Sandscapes** series (Smartscapes Ltd.). Go to www.cornertolearn.co.uk for more details. There are some excellent ideas for extending this theme in **Sandscapes 2 - Gardens**. There is a garden-scape and ideas card for creating a fantasy garden using the starting point of the rhyme *Mary, Mary, quite contrary* (*Sandscapes Garden Card, 2*).
- Explore the idea of creepie crawlies in the garden, and camouflage (*Sandscapes Garden Card, 3*).
- Create a shapes and pattern garden (*Sandscapes Garden Card, 4*).

Poems, stories and rhymes

If Only..., Neil Griffiths (Red Robin Books)
Doing the Garden, Sarah Garland (Puffin Books)
Rosie's Garden, Elizabeth Laird and Satomi Ichikawa (Mammoth)
The tale of the turnip (Traditional)
Mary, Mary, quite contrary (Traditional)
This Little Puffin, Elizabeth Matterson (Penguin Books) has an entire section on rhymes relating to gardens.

Creating ponds

- This could be an extension of a theme relating to gardens, water, change or in response to a poem or a story.

What resources will I need?

- large water tray or small, individual plastic fish tanks or washing-up bowls (It is better if the sides are transparent as children love looking at what is under the water.)
- stones, small rocks, pebbles and logs
- artificial water lilies (available from the garden pond area of most garden centres), or green plastic cut into water lily shapes, used with artificial flowers
- artificial water weed (found in aquarium shops / centres)
- water creatures - frogs, fish, dragonflies, snails (The *Early Learning Centre* sells a set which has the stages of development of a frog from a tadpole; use this with some bubble wrap to represent the frog spawn and the life cycle of the frog is complete.)
- set of ducks

" Take a young child out for a walk after a rainstorm and they will seek out puddles to splash in. "

Main activity

- Find out what the children already know about ponds. Look at pictures of ponds and pond environments. Do any children have them in their garden?
- Talk about safety issues relating to water.
- Look at the resources. If you have the life cycle of the frog, talk about this and look at pictures.
- Talk about dragonflies and their life cycle.
- Name all the resources and discuss how they might be used.
- Encourage the children to talk to an adult about their pond ideas before they start their play.
- Display pictures and photos about ponds and pond life. After they have created their ponds, get them to show them to the others and talk about what they have done. Adults in this area can encourage and extend vocabulary and introduce information about pond life.

Key learning opportunities

Communication, language and literacy

- Extend vocabulary, learning new words and their meaning.
- Use language to recreate roles and experiences.
- Use talk to clarify and express ideas and feelings.
- Interact with others.
- Retell rhymes and jingles.
- Speak confidently in front of others. (Talk about their pond creations.)

Personal, social and emotional development

- Work as part of a group.
- Be confident to try new activities.

Mathematical development

- Count reliably to ten.
- In practical activities, begin to use vocabulary involved in adding and subtracting (number rhymes, etc.).
- Learn vocabulary such as *bigger than*, *more than*, *as big as*, and so on.

Knowledge and understanding

- Find out about the world we live in.
- Find out about and identify some features of living things.
- Look closely at similarities, differences, pattern and change.
- Find out about different environments.

Physical development

- Handle tools and objects with increasing control.

Creative development

- Play imaginatively.

- Rhymes which reinforce number can be played out with resources such as the ducks and frogs. Favourites such as *Five little ducks went swimming one day* and *Five little speckled frogs sat on a speckled log eating some most delicious bugs, yum, yum,* are much more fun if you can actually play out the rhyme in your very own pond.

Extending the activity

- Read a story such as *Dear Greenpeace*. This is a dialogue between a little girl and *Greenpeace* about a whale she imagines has got stranded in her pond. It raises some environmental issues which can be discussed with the children. Children can be encouraged to make up their own pond stories as they play and draw pictures of their ideas.
- There may be a school pond or a park pond nearby to visit.
- Use a magnetic fishing game in the pond. There are games now that use plastic fish with magnets in them which will be very suitable for water play. This game is great for number work, hand-eye control – great fun if one is fishing in real water!

Poems, stories and rhymes

Dear Greenpeace, Simon James (Walker Books)
'Five speckled frogs', This Little Puffin, Elizabeth Matterson (Penguin Books)
Five little ducks (Traditional)
One, two, three, four, five, once I caught a fish alive, (Traditional)
The trouble with tadpoles, Sam Godwin (M.Y. Bees)

An under-the-sea garden

- This gives children a wonderful opportunity to develop their imaginations. It could be part of the theme Gardens, but could also follow stories such as **The Rainbow Fish**, **Sally and the Limpet** and **A house for Hermit crab**.
- It could be part of the follow-up to a seaside visit.

What resources will I need?

- large water tray or small plastic tanks (It is better if the sides are transparent as children love looking at what is under the water.)
- collections of brightly-coloured stones, pebbles, beads, large sequins, sequin waste, glittery plastic Christmas baubles
- shells, coral, small pieces of rock and stones
- artificial water weed and flowers
- castle or sunken shipwreck model (These can be bought in shops which sell equipment for aquariums.)
- plastic sea creatures, plastic mermaid
- small selection of off-cuts of drain pipe or similar (Builders often have these.)
- toy submarine
- selection of small boats

Main activity

- Start with a story, poem or similar.
- Look at the resources with the children. Look at some under-the-sea pictures.
- Talk about what they see. How many things can they name? Encourage the children to ask questions about what they see and to learn new vocabulary. Stress that this underwater garden can be as imaginative as they like.
- Encourage the children to show the rest of the group their underwater garden and talk about what they have done and who it is for.
- Display pictures and books about under the sea.

Key learning opportunities

Communication, language and literacy

- Extend vocabulary, learning new words and their meaning.
- Use language to recreate roles and experiences.
- Ask and answer questions.
- Describe their gardens to others.
- Become familiar with the printed word (looking at and sharing books such as *The Rainbow Fish*).

Personal, social and emotional development

- Work as part of a group.
- Be confident to try new activities.

Knowledge and understanding

- Find out about and identify some features of living things.
- Look closely at similarities, differences, pattern and change.

Physical development

- Handle tools and objects with increasing control.

Creative development

- Play imaginatively.

Extending the activity

- By adding a few extra resources, the children could create a playground for the sea creatures or mermaids. These resources could include small amounts of plastic building equipment such as Mobilo or Lego, cotton reels, small containers, string, etc.
- Children could tell stories about their sea garden and draw pictures.
- Introduce **Sandscapes 1 - Under the Sea** scene.

Poems, stories and rhymes

The Rainbow Fish series of stories, Marcus Pfister (North South) (There is also a *Rainbow Fish Storysack*, Storysack Ltd)
A house for Hermit Crab, Eric Carle (Puffin)
Sally and the Limpet, Simon James (Walker Books)
This little Puffin, Elizabeth Matterson (Penguin Books) has a number of rhymes relating to the water and sea creatures.

Using garden tools and resources for sand or water play

- Explore tools and equipment used for gardening. This is a simple activity to resource and set up. It encourages children to explore sieving, digging, raking, planting, moulding, pouring and filling. The sand can be either damp or dry.

What resources will I need?

- large sand tray, large water tray or a piece of garden
- collection of plastic flower pots of different sizes and shapes
- plastic watering can
- buckets
- set of small garden tools – a trowel, a fork, a rake, a sieve
- small seed planters (the type with very small compartments for individual seeds and small plants) and small seed trays
- plastic label sticks

❝ Children need to explore resources freely and develop their own play and ideas. ❞

Main activities

- There are several activities that can be developed from these resources. The children will need to look at the resources available with an adult and suggest how they can be used.
- First, let the children explore the flower pots in either the water or the sand. Assign an adult to the area so that some discussion can take place.
- Keep the sand dry and just allow the children to fill the flower pots and watch the sand flow through the holes. Choose flower pots of different sizes and with a different number of holes. Let the children count the holes and watch the same number of streams of sand water pour out from the bottom.
- Explore the idea of pushing the flower pots down in damp sand or water. Discuss what happens. In damp sand. Children can use the pots as moulds and dig and shape with the small garden tools.They can compare the sizes of the moulds and find out how many small pots it takes to fill a big pot. They can use the sand as earth and plant pretend flowers, etc. that they have made from recycled materials.

Key learning opportunities

Communication, language and literacy

- Extend vocabulary, learning new words and their meaning.
- Use language to recreate roles and experiences.
- Use talk to clarify and express ideas and feelings.
- Interact with others.

Personal, social and emotional development

- Work as part of a group.
- Be confident to try new activities.
- Be interested and excited and motivated to learn.

Mathematical development

- Count reliably to ten.
- Talk about and recognise different shapes and patterns.

- Learn vocabulary such as *bigger*, *greater*, *smaller*, *as big as*, and so on.
- Use words to describe position.
- Begin to understand ideas related to quantity and volume such as *holds more*, *holds less*, etc.

Knowledge and understanding

- Explore new materials and objects.
- Find out and identify some features of living things (plants, flowers, etc.).

Physical development

- Handle tools and objects with increasing control.

Creative development

- Play imaginatively.

Extending the activities

- If an adult can be present, encourage the children to try to put the pots and the moulds in order of size. Ask questions such as *Which is the biggest pot? Can you find the next biggest? Can you put them in an order, the biggest first and the smallest last?*
- A lot of early mathematical vocabulary and concepts can be introduced through this play. The play also offers opportunities for staff to observe and assess individual children's use of vocabulary and their understanding of early concepts such as size, amount, number, and so on.
- Use the seed trays and let the children make pretend plants to put in them. Let the children label the plants in their own way - emergent writing or a picture. Let them water their plants with the watering can.
- Plant some real seeds in trays with compost in and watch them grow.

Poems, stories and rhymes

Sam plants a sunflower, Katy Petty and Axel Scheffler (Macmillan Children's Books)

Jasper's Beanstalk, Nick Butterworth and Mick Inkpen (Hodder Children's Books)

Poems and rhymes from *This Little Puffin*, Elizabeth Matterson (Penguin Books)

5 At home and far away

- Sand and water play provides excellent opportunities for learning about environments. There are very good ideas for this type of play available from **Smartscapes Ltd**. The ideas come with a scape that can be used in the sand. Currently the scapes come in sets of three, with four ideas cards to each scape:

Environment: ***Jungle, Mountain and Under the Sea***

Urban: ***High Street, Building Site and Garden***

Out and About: ***Farmyard, Zoo, Seaside***

Transport: ***Airport, Garage, Harbour***

The Sea: Looking at boats

- The *Smartscape Sandscape* sets look at the sea and harbours, but the play is largely focused on work in the sand, so this section will focus on water play around the theme of sea and rivers.

What resources will I need?

- large water tray
- collection of different boats (There are several educational catalogues which sell collections of small boats. Try to find different types: sailing boats, fishing boats, yachts, speed boats, tugs, liners, cargo vessels, aircraft carriers, etc.)
- nets for the fishing vessels (The nets that citrus fruits are sold in are good for this.)
- construction sets such as *Mobilo* and *Lego*
- collection of junk materials for the children to make their own boats (plastic containers, polystyrene trays, corks , straws, paper, thin material, etc.)

Key learning opportunities

Communication, language and literacy

- Extend and learn new vocabulary.
- Use language to recreate roles and experiences.
- Use talk to clarify and express ideas and feelings.
- Interact with others.

Personal, social and emotional development

- Work as part of a group.
- Be confident to try new activities.
- Be interested and excited and motivated to learn.

Mathematical development

- Talk about and recognise different shapes and patterns.
- Learn vocabulary such as *bigger than*, *as big as*, *little*, etc. in relation to the size and shapes of the boats.

- Use words to describe position.
- Begin to understand ideas related to quantity and volume such as *holds more*, *holds less*, etc.

Knowledge and understanding

- Find out about the world we live in.
- Begin to understand how some things work.
- Begin to understand some scientific ideas such as floating and sinking.

Physical development

- Handle tools and objects with increasing control.

Creative development

- Play imaginatively.

Main activity

- Look at a book such as *I Love Boats*, Flora McDonnell (Walker Books).
- Look at pictures of different kinds of boats.
- Find out through questions what the children already know about boats.
- Look at the resources together.
- Initially, let the children play with the boats in the water.
- After a period of free play, assign an adult to the activity. Ask the children questions such as *How can you make the boats move in the water without touching them?*
- Let them experiment with blowing and flapping them along. Have a boat race. Do some boats move better than others? Are any of the boats more stable than others?
- Explore floating and sinking. Can they make the boats sink? Do they all sink in the same way? How many things do they need to put in their boat before it sinks?
- Read the story of *Mr Gumpy's Outing*, John Burningham (Red Fox).

Extending the activity

- Suggest the children design and make their own boats with junk materials. Ask them to try and make them so that they will float. Test the boats in the water tray. Discuss why some floated better than others. Extend this play to construction activities and encourage children to build boats. Let the children make boats out of big cardboard boxes in the role play area and dress up as fishermen, pirates, sailors, and so on.

Poems, stories and rhymes

I Love Boats, Flora MacDonald (Walker Books)
Row Your Boat, Pippa Goodhart (Mammoth)
The Journey, Neil Griffiths (Red Robin Books)
Mr Gumpy's Outing, John Burningham (Red Fox)
One Blue Boat, a counting rhyme, Linda Hammond (Picture Puffin)

The Sea: Pirates

Starting point

- Work around the theme of the sea, or a pirate story can be the starting point for fantasy play around adventure on the high seas. It can involve both water play and sand play.

- If you are very brave, sand and water could be used together in a large tray. Put a bowl / tank / small tray of water into a large sand tray to represent the sea. The water will provide anchorage and play with the pirate ship, while the sand will provide desert island play.

What resources will I need?

Pirates on the high seas:

- water tray or similar
- ship, a rowing boat
- treasure chest
- small boxes

Pirates on a desert island:

- a sand tray
- stones, foliage, fir cones, pebbles
- small treasure chest, treasure
- small skull and cross bones flag

Buried treasure game:

- collection of magnets
- treasure that is metal which will be attracted to the magnets
- good selection of pirates (pirate accessories set, which includes a treasure chest, barrels, boxes, canons and canon balls from the Early Learning Centre)
- illustrated seascape with a play mat
- pirate ship and pirate fort (designed for play without water)

Main activity

- Spend some time talking about pirates. Read some pirate stories such as **The man whose mother was a pirate**, Margaret Mahy (Puffin Books).

- Look at the resources together. Let the children explore the resources and play freely, making up their own pirate adventures as they play.

- Creating a pirate island will require the sand to be damp so that the children can mould contours and create areas of vegetation and rock.

- After a period of free play, suggest the children bury their treasure chest and get other members of the group to guess where it might be.

Key learning opportunities

Communication, language and literacy

- Extend vocabulary.
- Use language to recreate roles and experiences.
- Use talk to clarify and express ideas and feelings.
- Interact with others.

Personal, social and emotional development

- Work as part of a group.
- Be confident to try new activities.
- Be interested and excited and motivated to learn.

Knowledge and understanding

- Explore new materials using senses.
- Find out about the world we live in.
- Find out about some features of their world.

Physical development

- Handle tools and objects with increasing control.

Creative development

- Play imaginatively.

Extending the activity

- Introduce the children to magnets. Hide a collection of metal 'treasure' in the sand. Suggest they find it using the magnets. Tell the children how many pieces are buried so that the activity can involve some number work and also so that pieces are not left to rust in the damp sand.
- Let the children dress up as pirates for the sand and water play. (Pirate dressing-up gear is available from the *Early Learning Centre* and other toy shops.)
- Take the pirate play into other activity areas. Build pirate ships with construction kits, large cardboard boxes and junk modelling materials.
- Turn the role play area into a pirate ship. (See a **Corner to Learn**, Neil Griffiths (Nelson Thornes) for further ideas on this.)
- Play with small figures and models on play mats.
- Have a treasure hunt outside.
- Make pirate hats, flags and treasure maps.
- Remember to look at other ideas for play relating to the sea, seaside, harbours, etc. in the Smartscape series.

Poems, stories and rhymes

My Granny was a Pirate, Margaret Mahy (Puffin Books)
One-eyed Jake, Pat Hutchin (Puffin Books)
The big ship sails on the alley alley oh! (Traditional)
Jolly Roger, Colin McNaughton (Walker Books)

The Sea: Cold seas and lands

Starting point

- This theme is often explored as a follow-up to a story such as ***Polar bear, polar bear, what do you hear?***, Eric Carle and Bill Martin (Henry Holt and Co). It is an activity mainly for the water tray.

What resources will I need?

- large water tray with a small amount of water
- rocks and stones
- white polythene boxes
- large, white, square or oblong candles
- sheets of white plastic
- bubble wrap
- cotton wool
- silvery white pebbles (the sort used in flower arranging or fish tanks)
- shaving foam can be used to create a realistic snowy look and soon dissolves in the water (Large, non-crumbly polystyrene blocks can be used, but generally not recommended for children under five; **any crumbly, small pieces of polythene should not be used at all.**)
- selection of sea creatures found in cold seas – whales, seals, walruses, polar bears, penguins, arctic foxes

Main activity

- Start with a story and a discussion about cold, icy lands. Look at pictures of the Arctic and Antarctic. Look at a globe and identify the North Pole and South Pole areas.

- Look at the resources. Discuss how they can be used. Talk about icebergs, ships that break the ice, explorers and the animals that live in these places. Can the children name the creatures? What do they know about them already?

- Encourage the children to create an icy, cold environment with the resources in the water tray. If there is only a small amount of water, they will be able to have both sea and ice environments.

Key learning opportunities

Communication, language and literacy

- Enjoy listening to and using spoken language.
- Listen with enjoyment to story rhymes, etc. and make up their own. This is relevant if the story is used as a starting point.
- Extend vocabulary.
- Use language to recreate roles and experiences.
- Use talk to clarify and express ideas and feelings.

Personal, social and emotional development

- Work as part of a group.
- Be confident to try new activities.
- Be interested and excited and motivated to learn.
- Understand about important events in our lives and in the lives of others.

Mathematical development

- Learn vocabulary such as *bigger than*, *more than*, *as big as*, and so on.

Knowledge and understanding

- Explore new materials using senses.
- Find out about the world we live in.
- Learn about different environments.

Physical development

- Handle tools and objects with increasing control.

Creative development

- Play imaginatively.

Extending the activity

- Put real ice into the water tray so that the children can watch it melt. The ice can be coloured with small amounts of food colouring or the cubes frozen with small objects in them so that the children can see the objects emerge as the thawing process takes place. This is a good introduction to the concept of change.

- Cold, icy scenes can be created out of water using white cloth as a background. Mashed potato which can be moulded and shaped provides an interesting material for children to use to create a snow scene. Use a small tray for this. It also doesn't matter if they eat it!

Poems, stories and rhymes

The Bear, Raymond Briggs (Red Fox)
Dear Greenpeace, Simon James (Walker Books)
Other environments are explored in the *Sandscapes Series*, Smartscapes Ltd. They include:

Farmyard
Seaside
Mountains
Jungle
High Street
Building Site
Garage
Airport
Harbour

Hot countries – the desert

- This is often explored after a visit to a zoo or a safari park as a result of seeing animals that come from the desert and other hot climates. However, as in the previous section, a story would be a good starting point or perhaps someone's holiday or a visitor from another country.

What resources will I need?

- large sand tray with plenty of dry sand
- creatures likely to be found in such climates – camels, snakes, lizards, spiders, scorpions
- sand-coloured rocks and stones
- model palm trees or materials to represent these
- small container for some water
- materials to make tents with
- jeeps and model human figures
- combs or rakes to make sand patterns
- sieves

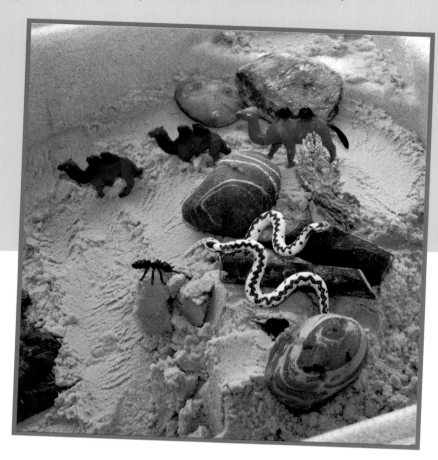

Main activity

- Show the children pictures of the desert. Show where the great deserts of the world are on the globe. Do the children know anything about deserts? What can they tell you? Do they know of any animals that live predominately in deserts? Look at the resources and discuss these. If possible, find some pictures of deserts so that the children can see how desolate they can be and how the wind blows the sand into amazing patterns and shapes.

- Talk about the people who live in deserts and how they live their lives. Introduce new vocabulary and its meaning such as *nomad*, *oasis*, etc.

- Look at pictures of tents and nomads living in the desert. Encourage the children to create their own desert landscape. Encourage them to make patterns in the dry sand with the combs and rakes. If very carefully supervised, they can experiment with blowing the sand through a straw to create wind blown patterns. Suggest that the creatures such as snakes, scorpions and spiders will want to hide away.

- Encourage the children to talk about what they are doing and to make up stories about their landscape.

Key learning opportunities

Communication, language and literacy

- Extend vocabulary.
- Use language to recreate roles and experiences.
- Enjoy listening to and using spoken language, using it in play and learning.
- Sustain attentive listening.
- Ask and answer questions confidently.

Personal, social and emotional development

- Work as part of a group.
- Be confident to try new activities.
- Be interested and excited and motivated to learn.
- Understand about important events in our lives and in the lives of others.

Mathematical development

- Talk about and recognise different shapes and patterns.

Knowledge and understanding

- Explore new materials using senses.
- Find out about the world we live in - different environments and cultures.

Physical development

- Handle tools and objects with increasing control.

Creative development

- Play imaginatively.

Extending the activity

- The **Sandscapes Series**, Smartscapes Ltd., has a wealth of ideas for extending this play to Jungle environments, the Zoo and Safari park. The series comes with scenery to provide a backdrop to the play.

Poems, stories and rhymes

Tallula's Atishoo!, Neil Griffiths (Red Robin Books)
Rumble in the Jungle, Giles Andreae and David Wojtowycz (Orchard Books)
Walking Through the Jungle, Stella Blackstone and Debbie Harter (Barefoot Books)

" Using books as a starting point for sand play will help children gain an understanding and insight into new environments. "

6 Fantasy play

 Starting point

Dinosaurs and dinosaur land

- Although not strictly complete fantasy, dinosaurs are a great fascination for young children. Play with natural materials and some dinosaur figures provides lots of opportunity to create fantasy landscapes and story scenarios.

What resources will I need?

- large sand tray or small trays for individual play (The sand will generally need to be damp so that contours can be moulded.)
- collection of model dinosaurs
- collection of natural materials – rocks, pebbles, stones, fir cones, foliage, bark, small logs
- small sand tools such as rakes, trowels and scoops
- simple pattern-making tools – combs, small moulds and shapes

Key learning opportunities

Communication, language and literacy

- Extend vocabulary, learn new vocabulary.
- Use language to recreate roles and experiences.
- Use talk to clarify and express ideas and feelings.
- Enjoy listening to and using spoken language.

Personal, social and emotional development

- Work as part of a group.
- Be confident to try new activities.
- Be interested, excited and motivated to learn.

Mathematical development

- Talk about and recognise different shapes and patterns.
- Learn vocabulary related to size and shape.

Knowledge and understanding

- Explore new materials using senses.
- Look closely at similarities and differences (comparing dinosaurs).
- Find out about the past.

Physical development

- Handle tools and objects with increasing control.

Creative development

- Play imaginatively.

Main activity

- It is quite possible that a number of children will know quite a lot about dinosaurs and will have already learnt to identify and name the most popular ones. Find out through questions what they already know.
- Look at reference books, pictures and stories about dinosaurs.
- Encourage the children to describe the sort of terrain they think the dinosaurs once lived in. Look at the resources and suggest that the children might like to make their own dinosaur land, using the natural materials and moulding the sand.
- Encourage the children to create hiding places for their dinosaurs – to rake, mould, scoop and press the sand into shapes to form a terrain. Introduce these words as they play.
- Encourage the children to talk about what they are doing and to make up their own stories as they play.

Extending the activity

- Create a dinosaur land in water. Put a small amount of water in the water tray. Make available a selection of natural materials such as rocks, stones, logs, etc. to create different levels and features. Suggest the children make a swamp – a watery environment for the dinosaurs.
- Adapt the story / rhyme *I'm going on a bear hunt* to *I'm going on a dinosaur hunt*.
- Suggest the children make a trail in the sand or outside which takes them through different landscapes to reach a dinosaur.
- Take dinosaurs into other areas – model-making, painting and drawing, creating a dinosaur cave outside or in the role play area.
- Make up dinosaur counting rhymes based on familiar rhymes such as *Ten green bottles* or *Five little speckled frogs*.

Poems, stories and rhymes

Dinosaurs and all that rubbish, Michael Foreman (Puffin Books)
Dinosaur Roar, Paul and Henrietta Stickland (Ragged Bears)
Dilly the Dinosaur, Tony Bradman (Mammoth)
Dinosaur Dreams, Alan Alhberg (Walker Books)

Going to the circus

- The children will need to have had some experience of a circus, either through a visit, a television programme or a story. The sand provides a very realistic material for the circus ring, although sawdust could be used even more realistically.

What resources will I need?

- collection of animals which might be used in a circus scene
- collection of figures
- small bricks to create the ring and seats for the spectators
- vehicles
- construction equipment to build structures for the trapeze and similar
- damp sand

> " Imaginative play with animals is always popular and is easy to resource. "

Main activity

- Find out what the children already know about the circus.
- Look at pictures of circuses.
- Read a circus story.
- Look at the resources and talk about how the circus is set up.
- Let the children play freely with the resources and talk about what they are doing and what is happening.
- Use appropriate opportunities to introduce new language such as *trapeze*, *ringmaster*, *big top*, and so on.
- Encourage the children to tell their circus stories to the others.

Extending the activity

- Invest in a circus play set. A colourful wooden set from *Insect Lore*, PO Box 1420, Kiln Farm, Milton Keynes MK19 6ZH comes with a big top, animals, clowns and spectators. It is ideal for imaginative play on a small scale on the floor or table top. It may spoil if used in the sand.
- Develop the whole idea of the circus, provide dressing-up clothes and turn the role play area into the big top. Use music such as *Barnum* for dance and movement.

Poems, stories and rhymes

Animal rhymes such as found in **This Little Puffin**, Elizabeth Matterson (Penguin Books)
Clown, Quentin Blake (Red Fox)
The Greatest Show on Earth, John Prater (Walker Books)

Key learning opportunities

Communication, language and literacy

- Extend vocabulary. Learn new words and their meaning.
- Use language to recreate roles and experiences.
- Use talk to clarify and express ideas and feelings.
- Interact with others.

Personal, social and emotional development

- Work as part of a group.
- Be confident to try new activities.
- Be interested, excited and motivated to learn.

Mathematical development

- Talk about and recognise different shapes and patterns.
- Learn vocabulary related to size, shape and comparison.

Knowledge and understanding

- Explore new materials using senses.
- Find out about the world we live in and the lives of other people, their beliefs and culture (circus life).

Physical development

- Handle tools and objects with increasing control.

Creative development

- Play imaginatively.

7 Traditional Stories

Starting point

Big Book Time

- There are many stories which lend themselves to being performed in the sand and water play areas. Favourites such as *Sleeping Beauty*, *Hansel and Gretel*, *Rapunzel*, *Snow White* and *Three Billy Goats Gruff* are just a few. It might be worthwhile creating a collection of resources which will fit with a variety of stories.

- The starting point will usually be the telling of a story or after sharing a Big Book with the children.

What resources will I need?

- materials to represent trees and vegetation to create forests or similar environments – green pan scourers, plastic greenery, model trees, real vegetation (to be renewed at each play session), fir cones, plastic flowers, oasis

- stones, pebbles, pieces of bark, small logs

- model figures (The *Early Learning Centre* sells small plastic figures around the theme of knights, princesses, etc. which would be ideal for this type of play.)

- castellated moulds

- cylindrical moulds

- small moulding and digging tools

- paper, pens and lollipop sticks to make flags

- extras can be added as appropriate to the story

Key learning opportunities

Communication, language and literacy

- Extend vocabulary.
- Use language to recreate roles and experiences.
- Enjoy listening and using language.
- Sustain listening and listen with enjoyment to stories and rhymes.
- Retell stories using the correct sequence of events.
- Make up own stories when playing imaginatively.

Personal, social and emotional development

- Work as part of a group.
- Be confident to try new activities.
- Be interested and excited and motivated to learn.

Mathematical development

- Talk about and recognise different shapes and patterns.

Knowledge and understanding

- Explore new materials using senses.
- Find out about the world and other people.

Physical development

- Handle tools and objects with increasing control.

Creative development

- Play imaginatively, creating imaginative environments.

Main activity

- Tell the story. Talk about what the children recall – the characters, the scenes, etc.
- Look at the resources together. Encourage the children to explore the materials freely and create their own scenes and environments. This can be done in individual trays or as a group in a large sand tray. The sand will need to be damp.
- Encourage the children to tell their part of the story and to share their work with others. Recalling and retelling a story is an important part of children's language development and if adults are able to observe this play, they will gain valuable information relating to children's progress and understanding.

Extending the activity

- The children can make up their own stories and scenes. The play can take place on the floor or table top with a similar collection of figures and resources. A construction set can be included to facilitate the making of castles, houses, etc.

Poems, stories and rhymes

Traditional fairy stories
There was a princess long ago in ***This Little Puffin***, Elizabeth Matterson (Penguin Books)
Winnie Wagtail, ***Ringo the Flamingo***, ***The Journey***, ***Itchy Bear***, ***If Only...***, Neil Griffiths (Red Robin Books)

Other stories and rhymes

- There are many favourite stories and rhymes which lend themselves to imaginative play in the sand and water. The **Sandscapes Series**, Smartscapes Ltd., has a wide range of ideas for using story as a starting point for imaginative play in the sand and water. The colourful scapes provide a great background for the play and also provide lots of opportunity for discussion.

- **Sandscapes** provide ideas for work with the following stories and rhymes:

The Very Hungry Caterpillar, Eric Carle (Puffin Books)
Creepie crawlies in the garden, Garden card, 3
Mary, Mary, Quite Contrary (a fantasy garden),
Garden card, 2
The Rainbow Fish, Marcus Pfister (North South Books)
A fantasy underwater world, Under the sea card, 2
Rumble in the Jungle, Giles Andreae and
David Wojowrycz (Orchard)
Creating a jungle environment, Jungle card 1
Mr Gumpy's Motor Car, John Burningham (Red Fox)
An adventure with a car, Garage card, 3
The Lighthouse Keeper's Lunch, Rhonda and David
Armitage (Reading Hippo)
*Creating the journey of the lighthouse keeper's lunch
from the cottage to the lighthouse*, Harbours card, 3
Rosie's Walk, Pat Hutchins (Red Fox)
Making Rosie's trail across the farmyard, Farm card, 4

- Stories such as **Rosie's Walk** provide a great opportunity for children to create trails in the sand and other materials. It is a valuable activity for helping children to sequence the events of a story and retell narrative.

- Other stories and rhymes which lend themselves to this are:

We're all Going on a Bear Hunt, Michael Rosen and Helen Oxenbury (Walker Books) This story can be recreated by using a collection of small trays, each one containing a different material to represent the different environments the hunters encountered. Children could make up their own stories based on the idea of a trail or a track and meeting others on the way.

The Gingerbread Boy (Traditional)

Chicken Licken (Traditional)

The Journey, Neil Griffiths (Red Robin Books)

Having a picnic, Sarah Garland (Puffin Books)

Alex's Outing, Mary Dickinson (Hippo Reading)

Incey Wincey spider – play out the rhyme with a collection of pipes and plastic spiders. Learn about the force of water.

Ten Green Bottles – use plastic green bottles to play this rhyme. It is a pouring and filling activity. Children learn about *full*, *empty*, *half empty*, etc.

The Owl and the Pussycat – boats and island fantasy play.

Where the wild things are, Maurice Sendak (Harper Collins)

8 Outdoor Play

- Outside on a warm day or with children well wrapped up if the weather is cooler, is the ideal space for play with natural materials. However, a few safety rules need to be considered.

- If the weather is hot, ensure that the children are in a shady place with sun hats and sun cream on. Ensure outdoor sand pits are kept covered when not in use. The latest outdoor sand pits have sonic cat scarers built in which takes away the need to keep them covered. Inspect them regularly for debris and unwanted, potentially dangerous bits and pieces.

- Always ensure that children are supervised when playing with sand and water outside. Keep water clean and debris free.

Sand play outside

- Many of the suggestions offered early in this book can be played outside, but there are some activities that lend themselves better to outdoor's play. Play in a large sand pit is more like playing on the beach and can involve children in making large sand structures, excavating and digging deep holes, making tunnels and laying pipes and generally exploring sand on a larger scale.

- Give children large resources such as planks, drain pipes, large building site toys such as diggers, dumper trucks, buckets, wooden or plastic bricks (not your best sets as these spoil in the sand, but an old collection will provide endless exploration and fun).

- Ensure children are aware of all the rules for sand play and do not throw sand or equipment.

- Ensure children are suitably clad with wellingtons, bare feet or other suitable foot gear.
- Let children explore resources freely, but some great themes can be investigated and developed such as The Building Site, Castles, Holes in Sand and Patterns in Sand. Resources can be adapted to fit the larger scale of play.

Water play outdoors

- Water play outside can free Early Years practitioners from the chore of ensuring that water play does not soak everything in sight! Outside, the children can play more freely and use different equipment and have different experiences.

Paint and painting

- Give children buckets and clean, paint cans filled with water, paint roller trays with water in and a selection of paint rollers and different sized brushes. They will have great fun 'painting' the outside walls of the building, the playground and making pictures and patterns before the water dries. Stress that this must only be done with water as no one is going to appreciate multi-coloured walls and playground. This activity gives children the chance to work on a big area, to explore the concept of evaporation and to create their own water designs.

Puddles

- Create puddles on the playground and let the children ride bikes and other wheeled vehicles through the water. They are fascinated by the patterns that this creates and quickly learn how to control the vehicle to create a variety of lines and paths. Chalk around the puddles so that children can see evaporation taking place. Name the puddles! Children can then learn to follow simple directions, e.g. ride round Fat Puddle, through Squiggly Puddle, by Long Puddle and stop in the middle of Tiny Puddle.

Pumps and sprays

Outside is the perfect environment for experimenting with pumps and sprays. Using a variety of pumps and sprays, children can see which sprays the furthest. Can they make patterns with the sprays? What kind of patterns are they – wiggly, straight, round, curved?

Washing

- Erect a clothes line. Give the children big bowls of water and some dolls' clothes or real clothes to wash. Make sure detergents are mild and suitable for children who may have allergies. Talk about the process of washing. Give the children pegs to hang out the washing and a clothes basket to gather it back in again. Discuss drying times – do some things take longer than others?

Bathing dolls

Put out baby baths and a collection of dolls and the resources in the section 'Bathing the baby'. Outside, this activity can be as messy as the children like!

Picnics

Allow water with the picnic sets and tea sets outside. It is much more fun to pour out real liquid from the teapot or the squash bottle.

Key learning opportunities

Communication, language and literacy

- Extend vocabulary.
- Use language to recreate roles and experiences.
- Use talk to clarify and express ideas and feelings.
- Interact with others.

Personal, social and emotional development

- Work as part of a group.
- Be confident to try new activities.
- Be interested and excited and motivated to learn.

Mathematical development

- Talk about and recognise different shapes and patterns.
- Learn vocabulary such as *bigger than*, *more than*, *as big as*, and so on.

- Learn language relating to position, direction and order.

Knowledge and understanding

- Explore new materials using senses.
- Find out about the world we live in – creating environments.

Physical development

- Handle tools and objects with increasing control.
- Move with confidence, imagination and safety.

Creative development

- Play imaginatively on a large scale.

Other materials

Other materials that can be used outside to their best advantage are mud, collections of stones (emphasise the dangers of throwing these – if in doubt, do not include them!), cement, clay, gravel, leaf mould, bark, twigs, small logs and shells. Some of these materials, such as the cement, will need adult supervision. Of course, do not forget the opportunities a patch of earth provides for digging, planting and watering.

Safety

Frequent references, where and when appropriate, have been made throughout this book to the safety aspects of play. Play workers will need to check that any materials they use either in conjunction with the sand and water or on their own are safe for the children to use.

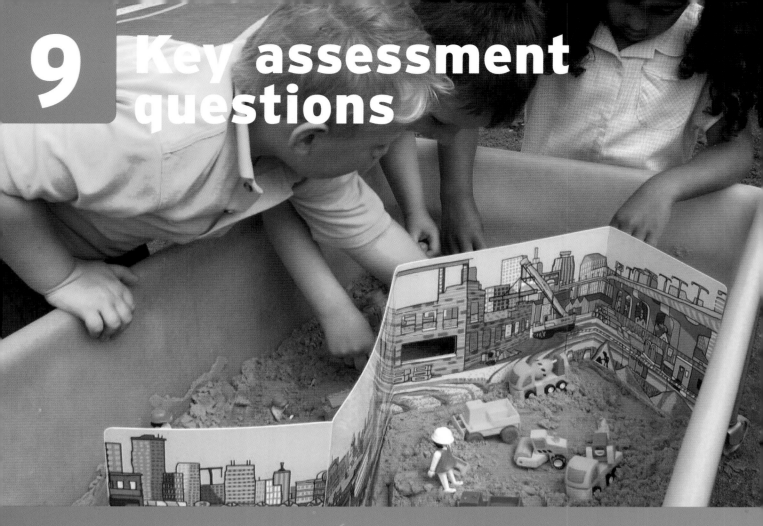

9 Key assessment questions

Personal, social and emotional development

- Do the children have an understanding that other children need to be considered, e.g. that equipment and space needs to be shared and that taking turns is important?

- Is there an understanding that actions have consequences, e.g. throwing sand can hurt others?

- Can they put equipment away?

- Do they help others?

- Are they helpful and patient, e.g. helping someone else to rebuild a collapsed sand castle?

- Do they appreciate and comment on the experience of playing with these materials, e.g. remarking on textures, and sensory experiences?

- Are they confident in their play?

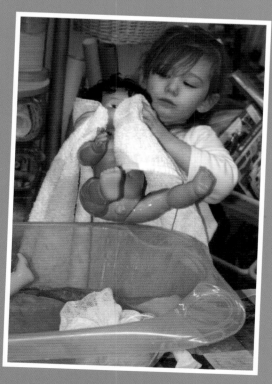

Communication, language and literacy

- Do they use and know a range of descriptive words relating to the sand and water?
- Do they listen to others?
- Do they talk to the others while playing – discuss the materials, share feelings and ideas, negotiate for the use of tools space, etc.?
- Do they talk about what they are doing and make up stories and fantasy situations with the resources?
- Can they retell a story when playing with small imaginative play resources in the sand and water?
- Do they make marks and patterns with the tools in a controlled way?

Mathematical development

- Do they know and use some mathematical language correctly, e.g. *bigger than, smaller than, empty, full, half empty, half full*?
- Can they describe and make different shapes and patterns?
- Can they make some estimations? E.g. *I think 10 scoops will fill the bucket.*
- Can they count, e.g. count the number of scoops using correct number names and one-to-one correspondence?
- Can they sort materials, e.g. all the spiral shells, all the equipment which holds water?
- Can they measure? E.g. 6 cups of water fill the bowl.

Knowledge and understanding of the world

- Do they comment on and question change, remarking on similarities and differences e.g. when water is added to dry sand, when water is made soapy?
- Are they beginning to understand the different properties of the different materials?
- Do they try to solve problems, e.g. using the funnel to fill containers with small apertures?
- Can they make some predictions? E.g. *I think this might float*.
- Do they ask questions about why things happen? E.g. *Why does the sand wheel turn with dry sand and water but not with wet sand?*

Physical development

- Can they successfully handle the larger tools such as spades, buckets, sand wheels, etc.?
- Are they beginning to develop fine manipulative skills such as placing shells, small stones, flags, etc. on sand castles, filling containers with water, pouring water from one container to another?
- Are they developing some spatial awareness, e.g. aware of others playing in the same area?
- Do they experiment and test new tools and equipment, e.g. pumps and sprays, funnels and sieves?

Creative development

- Do they create different effects with tools and materials, making patterns and pictures?
- Do they play imaginatively, e.g. making a seascape scene, a building site scene?
- Do they create different environments using tools and hands, e.g. mountains, rivers, ponds?
- Do they enjoy being creative?
- Do they appreciate and value the creations of others, e.g. commenting on a beautiful sand castle, a pretty pattern?

These are just a few of the questions which might be asked in the course of assessing children's development when playing with natural materials. Of course, you will not be concentrating on all areas of learning at once and will only want to do focused observation from time to time. However, with a number of adults working in settings for young children, there will be times when someone notices something significant in a child's play and they may wish to record this. A simple way to do incidental recording is to place stickers and pens in the areas so that if an adult notices something significant, they can make a quick note, stick it on a board or similar and transfer it to any record documents later.

Adults may wish to keep a simple record which identifies the theme or purpose of the play and asks questions such as:

- What did the child enjoy most?
- What milestones were reached?
- Were there any significant moments during the play?

10 Information for parents

- Parents often ask questions relating to the value of play in the sand and water. It is sometimes difficult for parents to understand the value of this play. Parents of young children often appreciate ideas for how they can introduce children to play with natural materials at home. The following pages can be photocopied to give to parents who require more information on play with sand and water.

Play with sand and water

Overview

- Few young children can resist playing with water, sand, mud or other similar materials. Go for a walk after a rainstorm and your child will seek out the puddles to splash in. Try to do the washing-up and suddenly there is an eager little helper at your elbow. Go to do some gardening and someone is just behind you doing their own bit of digging. Play with these materials is very absorbing and great fun. It does not require expensive equipment and your child learns from the experience. This information sheet looks at ways in which you can provide this kind of play for your child and help them learn at the same time.

What can my child learn from this kind of play?

- Play with sand and water helps children's physical development. Through lifting, pouring, sieving, sifting, filling, emptying and handling these materials children learn to control movement, particularly those movements requiring careful hand and eye coordination. Filling one container from another can be quite tricky and require a lot of practice. Children who have lots of practice with these sort of activities often find it easier to control pencils, crayons and paintbrushes when they go to school.

- Play with sand and water is pleasurable. It is calming and relaxing to explore the feel, smell, and movement of these materials and, through doing this, children make discoveries which will be important to them when learning scientific things at school. They learn how these materials behave in different situations. They begin to understand that, for example, sand behaves differently when it is wet from when it is dry. Wet sand can be moulded and shaped, while dry sand behaves a bit like water and can flow and be moved easily. They discover that some things float on water, while some sink. They find out that materials sometimes change in certain conditions: water can become ice; too much water in the sand and you won't be able to mould it; put lots of stones in your bucket of water and it will overflow. These are all important steps towards later scientific understanding.

- With some help from you, children will learn lots of new words and their meaning in this play. Some of the language will be essential to their understanding in maths. Words such as *full*, *empty*, *half full*, *half empty*, *more*, *less*, *fewer*, *big*, *little*, etc. will naturally come into conversation. It is fun to encourage some counting in this play. You might ask questions such as:

  How many yoghurt pots of water / sand does it take to fill the bucket?
  Can you put four flags on your castle?
  Can you make three sand pies?

- There are many other words your child will learn if you are able to play sometimes too: in water play, words such as *pour*, *flow*, *trickle*, *gush*, *spill*, *overflow*, *gurgle*, *float*, *sink*, *leak* and *dribble*; in sand play, words such as *tip*, *scoop*, *scrape*, *shape*, *mould*, *crumble*, *firm*, *loose*, *dry*, *heap*, *burrow*, *tunnel*, *hole* and *pit*.

Things to use

- You don't need expensive sand trays and water equipment. For water play, bath time and washing-up are good times to show your child what you can do with water, but you can also give them a large bowl of water to play with on the floor on a large plastic mat or sheet, or best of all, outdoors in summer. Do remember: **NEVER LEAVE A SMALL CHILD ALONE WITH WATER.**

- For sand play, plastic seed trays, bowls, boxes, an old paddling pool or sand on a large plastic sheet will provide a perfectly adequate container for sand. There will be many things in your own home and garden which will make play fun.

- Some things can be used with both sand and water: sieves, funnels, old spoons, plastic containers, plastic pipes and tubing, straws, washing-up liquid bottles, rubber gloves, colander, empty spray containers (as used for window cleaners, etc,) bubble pipes, corks, stones, sticks, pebbles, shells, fir cones, lolly sticks, liquid soap pumps, etc.

Things to do with water

- Help to wash the car and wash up.
- Have a toys' tea party with water in the teapot and a bowl to wash up in afterwards.
- Wash dolls' clothes and hang them on a small washing line at child height.
- Bath the dolls - remember to provide real things like soap, a flannel, a towel, etc.
- Water the garden.
- Provide coloured water (use food colourings).
- On a warm day, put some ice in the water - let your child watch it melt. (You can also make coloured cubes of ice with food colouring.)
- Make and blow bubbles.
- See which things soak up water and which don't. (A small collection of things such as sponges, paper, cloth, wool, plastic, etc. will start an interesting investigation.)
- See which things will float and sink.
- Provide old guttering, pipes, etc. to make rivers and canals, and experiment with moving water with siphons, pumps. etc.
- Provide a bucket of water and paint brush and allow your child to paint or draw on suitable surfaces outside (as long as your child realises that they cannot do this with the real thing!).
- Let your child put suitable small toys in the water to create imaginative places, e.g. boats, ducks, frogs, water creatures, plastic pond weed, stones, rocks, shells, etc. Many toy shops sell collections of small plastic toys, such as sea creatures and pond creatures, and are inexpensive.

Things to do in sand

- Feel how wet, damp and dry sand are different.
- Mould and build with wet sand.
- Pour and sift dry sand.
- Pour sand from container to container.
- Fill up bigger containers from smaller containers and count.
- Make flags with paper and lolly sticks.
- Make a road for cars and other machinery.
- Make a building site with toy vehicles, stones, pebbles, matchboxes, twigs, etc.
- Make gardens in the sand using fir cones, stones, coloured pebbles, leaves, flower petals, twigs, etc.
- Let your child put suitable toys in the sand to create imaginative places. Farm animals, zoo animals, dinosaurs and creepie crawlies are all fun to use in the sand with some of the other natural things.
- Give your child a collection of things which make interesting patterns in sand - old combs, a piece of mesh, a potato masher, a flower pot, sticks, tubes, etc. Encourage your child to 'write' in sand, possibly write their name or practise making patterns with a stick, which will lead to writing later on.

A few tips on making it fun and safe

- Always remember it's got to be fun for you and your child - it may make a bit of a mess, so whenever possible keep it as an outdoor activity. Put them in old clothes and on a warm day, very little clothing is required, but **REMEMBER** the sun cream and sun hat. Wellingtons prevent wet feet, if this is going to be a problem.
- Be firm about not throwing sand. Explain the consequences to eyes, etc.
- Ensure all empty containers are well cleaned and free from any chemicals they once contained.
- Do not use washing-up liquid for bubbles - this can cause skin rashes and discomfort. A good alternative is baby bath liquid.
- Do not leave sand uncovered outside - animals like to use it for all sorts of unpleasant things.
- Always supervise water play - small children can drown in very little water.
- Finally, enjoy it. Have fun. Quite a lot of adults like playing with sand and water too and just need a good excuse to do it!

Conclusion

- Play with sand, water and other natural materials is totally absorbing for young children. From the youngest age, children are fascinated by the qualities and the mysteries of these materials. We have all seen the irresistable attraction of puddles and gutters for children and their delight in paddling, dancing in and out of a spray of water, having a bath and digging and moulding with sand and mud.

- This book, along with other ideas found in the *Sandscapes Series*, *Smartscape Ltd.*, gives some suggestions of how Early Years practitioners can foster and develop this natural enthusiasm for play with these materials and thus provide satisfying and absorbing play which will develop and extend all aspects of social, emotional and intellectual learning. It is hoped that children will sometimes be given the opportunity to play alone with these materials, sometimes in groups, and sometimes with adult participation and that early years settings will have systems in place to encourage children to make some decisions about what they will do and how they will do it.

Anne Pratt (B. Ed. Hons) taught in the primary sector for 24 years, specializing in the education of 3 - 8 year olds. She had headship experience in both a Nursery School and a Primary School. In 1988 she was appointed Early Years Adviser for The Wiltshire LEA and was responsible for developing and extending nursery provision throughout the county, supporting Early Years teachers and providing training for all those working with young children. Since her retirement in 1997 she has worked as an independent consultant, but derives most pleasure and satisfaction from helping her grandchildren learn through first hand experience, investigation and fun!

Acknowledgements

Many thanks go to the following for their help and support with this book:

Jill Lakeman, Clare Knight and all the children and staff of
  Start Point Sessional Nursery, Sholing, Southampton
Eldene Infant School, Swindon
Caia Park Nursery School, Wrexham
Roger Ogle, for the majority of the photography appearing
  in this book
Neil Griffiths and David Rose
My husband Alan, for his patience and invaluable help with
  computer skills.